SAUDI ARABIA

Cath Senker

W

FRANKLIN WATTS

LONDON • SYDNEY

Designer Rita Storey
Editor Sarah Ridley
Art Director Jonathan Hair
Editor-in-Chief John C. Miles
Picture research Diana Morris

First published in 2006 by Franklin Watts

Franklin Watts
338 Euston Road
London NW1 3BH

Franklin Watts Australia
Hachette Children's Books
Level 17/207 Kent Street
Sydney NSW 2000

A CIP catalogue record for this book
is available from the British Library.

Dewey classification number: 915.38

ISBN-10: 0 7496 6668 4
ISBN-13: 978 0 7496 6668 2

Printed in China

Franklin Watts is a division of Hachette Children's Books.

CONTENTS

SAUDI ARABIA OCCUPIES 80 PER CENT OF THE ARABIAN PENINSULA. *It is about the size of Western Europe but more than 95 per cent of the country is desert. In contrast to the desert, along the Red Sea coast there are forests and mountains and in the north-east and east of the country many salt flats are found. Saudi Arabia is the largest country in the world with no permanent rivers or freshwater lakes. Less than two per cent of the land can be used for farming.*

HIGHS AND LOWS

The climate is harsh in Saudi Arabia, with great extremes of temperature. Except in the mountains, it is normal for temperatures to reach a scorching 48 degrees between May and September although nights can be cold in the desert. In the winter, there can be frost and snow in the mountains and inland. In all seasons, strong winds can cause unpleasant sandstorms. Rainfall is rare – below 200 millimetres per year, and often less than half of that.

Riyadh is the capital city, home to about 3.5 million people. Other major cities are Jeddah, Makkah, Madinah and Dammam. The country is divided into 13 provinces.

THE PEOPLE

The population of Saudi Arabia in 2005 was 25.6 million, including 5.5 million non-Saudis. The population is growing extremely rapidly as Saudi women, on

These maps show Saudi Arabia's position in the world.

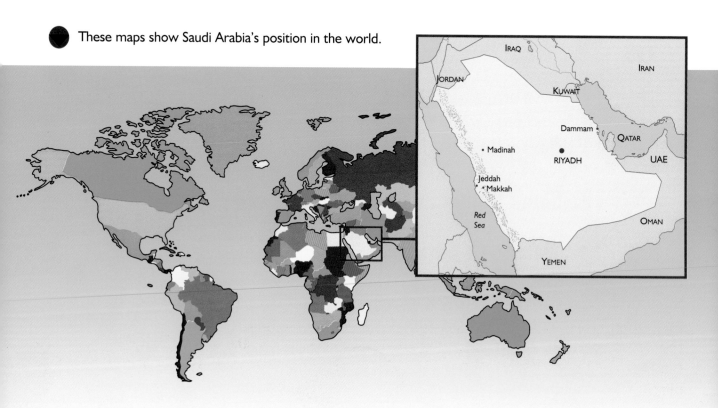

KNOW YOUR FACTS

In Saudi Arabia there are many oases, fertile areas of land that occur in a desert wherever a constant supply of water is available. The water comes from springs and wells under the ground. Date palms grow at oases. At the largest oasis, Al-Hasa (in eastern Saudi Arabia), there are about 12,000 hectares of palm groves with about 3 million date trees.

average, have six children each. The average age of the population is just 19. Ninety per cent of the Saudi people are Arabs.

IN THE NEWS

Several issues bring Saudi Arabia into the international news. With the largest oil reserves in the world, about a quarter of the world total, its oil is vital to the world economy. The country is also the site of the holiest places in Islam – Makkah and Madinah. So, every year, millions of pilgrims from all over the world visit the

Kingdom. Finally, Saudi Arabia is important internationally as a country friendly towards Western countries in the conflict-ridden Middle East. However, this friendly relationship causes tensions within the Kingdom, and opposition from radical Islamic groups has grown in recent years. Since 2003, some groups have carried out terrorist attacks within Saudi Arabia.

FOR THOUSANDS OF YEARS, THE ARABIAN PENINSULA, *including modern-day Saudi Arabia, was inhabited by nomadic tribes who farmed, hunted and herded their animals. Some important trade routes crossed the region so various civilisations influenced the people of Arabia. In 570 CE, the Prophet Muhammad, the Prophet of Islam, was born in Makkah. As an adult, he and his followers established the new religion of Islam, which spread across Arabia, the rest of the Middle East and into Europe.*

In the mid-18th century the Saud family joined forces with Muhammad Ibn Abd al-Wahhab, a Muslim reformer, to create a new state in part of Arabia. From 1902 Ibn Saud conquered the entire area that makes up the modern state of Saudi Arabia. He proclaimed the Kingdom of Saudi Arabia in 1932 and became King Abd al-Aziz Al-Saud.

OIL – "BLACK GOLD"

After the discovery of Saudi oil in 1938, a US company, the Arabian American Oil Company (Aramco), was formed in 1944 to help extract the oil. Through its ownership of the oil industry, the USA became the most influential foreign power in the country. (Saudi Arabia did not gain complete control of Aramco until 1980, when it was renamed Saudi Aramco.)

Saudi Arabia's fortunes were transformed by the new wealth from oil sales. Under Abd al-Aziz's successors, his son Saud (ruled 1953–1964) and then Saud's brother Faisal (1964–1975), the country modernised fast. Many people moved to the cities. There was a massive building programme to construct roads, schools, hospitals, apartment buildings and palaces.

In 1960 Saudi Arabia helped to found the Organisation of Petroleum Exporting Countries (OPEC) to coordinate the oil policies of member countries. During the

King Abd al-Aziz Al-Saud created Saudi Arabia as we know it today.

Cold War between the USSR and the USA, Saudi Arabia was on the USA's side. However, the Saudi government opposed the US policy of supporting Israel because of its sympathies with the Arab Palestinians. When the USA assisted Israel in the 1973 Arab-Israeli War, Saudi Arabia led the oil producers in a temporary boycott – they refused to sell oil to the USA, and the price of oil quadrupled.

In 1975 King Faisal was assassinated, and his half-brother Khalid became king. Four years into his reign, in 1979, rebels occupied the Great Mosque in Makkah in a dramatic challenge to the monarchy but they were defeated within a fortnight. Upon King Khalid's death in 1982, Prince Fahd became king.

From the 1970s, rapid economic and social development continued. There were vast improvements in health services, and free education was provided at all levels. However, in the mid-1980s, oil prices fell, and development slowed.

KNOW YOUR FACTS

Wealth from the oil industry has led to a rapid improvement in the standard of living in Saudi Arabia. In 1951, there were just 226 schools with 29,887 students. By 2005, there were over 24,000 schools with nearly 5 million students. The number of primary healthcare clinics has also grown from 51 in 1970 to over 3,300 in 2000.

An armed soldier guards an oil pipeline. Wealth from the sale of oil has transformed the desert kingdom since the 1930s.

MOST OF THE PEOPLE OF SAUDI ARABIA ARE ARABS, INCLUDING NOMADIC BEDOUIN ARABS. *Over the past 50 years, many Bedouin have settled permanently. Now less than 10 per cent of them keep their traditional nomadic lifestyle of moving from place to place to graze their camels, sheep, goats or cattle.*

There are also large numbers of foreign workers in the country – around a fifth of the population. Most are Arabs, Africans and Asians, along with a minority of Europeans and Americans. They work in every area of the economy.

RELIGION

Islam is the religion of Saudi Arabia and all Saudis are Muslim. The majority are Sunni Muslims who follow the Hanbali school of Islam, based on the theories of the 9th-century Islamic thinker, Ahmad Ibn Hanbal. His teachings became central to the Islamic reform movement of Abd al-Wahhab in the 18th century, which helped form the modern country of Saudi Arabia.

In the eastern part of the country, most people are Shi'a Muslims who make up around 15 per cent of the Saudi population. The split between Sunni and Shi'a Muslims dates back to the 7th century, when there was a disagreement over who should lead their community after the death of the Prophet Muhammad. However, both groups use the same Qur'an and share their Islamic beliefs.

 A group of Bedouin men share a sociable meal together, eating from a communal dish.

Saudi industry, such as this car factory, relies on large numbers of foreign workers.

A WAY OF LIFE

Islam is not just a religion but also a way of life in Saudi Arabia. Everyone is expected to observe the basic customs. Five times a day, Muslims are called to prayer – all businesses close and activities stop while people pray. Everyone is expected to dress modestly and women have to cover their hair, arms and legs in public. Alcohol and gambling are banned.

The Saudi rulers strongly believe that the Islamic spirit should be preserved in the birthplace of Islam. Migrant workers of different faiths are not allowed to practise their own religion. Saudis and foreigners do not live together. Westerners live in their own separate compounds, and their children attend separate schools.

GROUNDS FOR DEBATE

The Saudi government treats foreign workers as guests of Saudi Arabia, employed to do a particular job. Saudis and foreigners live separately as, if they mixed with local people, the government fears this would affect the Islamic nature of the Kingdom. It would become a multicultural, rather than a purely Muslim, society. Yet it can be argued that most countries have a mixture of peoples. Migrants arrive and naturally mix with the local population, producing a richer culture. What effects might combining cultures have? Would they be good or bad?

Pilgrims on their way to make the Hajj.

EVERY YEAR, DURING THE TWELFTH ISLAMIC MONTH, *around two million Muslims from all over the world make a pilgrimage to Saudi Arabia. They come to visit the holy sites of Makkah. It is the duty of all Muslims to try to make this journey at least once in their lifetime. The purpose of the pilgrimage is to stop all worldly activities for a few days and focus on Allah (God) alone.*

Male pilgrims change into simple white garments for the Hajj to show that they are all equal before God. Women wear white or plain dark garments. The pilgrims perform rituals to remember important events in the lives of the Prophets Ibrahim, Ismail and Muhammad. First, they attend the Ka'bah Mosque in Makkah. In the centre is the holy building, the Ka'bah, which Muslims believe is the oldest shrine to God. All Muslims worldwide face in the direction of the Ka'bah when they perform daily prayers.

Saudi Arabia has a Ministry of Hajj, which provides services for the pilgrims. It coordinates their arrival and arranges transport around the holy sites. There are enormous tent cities where pilgrims can stay while performing the rituals. Security forces control the crowds; this is a mammoth task.

HAJJ DEATHS

Despite careful planning, things can go disastrously wrong. In January 2006, tens of thousands of pilgrims were in Mina, a town near Makkah that is on the pilgrimage route. They were heading towards the three pillars that represent the devil. Here, the faithful throw seven stones at the pillars to cleanse them of their sins. As they rushed to complete the ritual, many tripped over baggage and fell. In the stampede, over 350 people were crushed to death.

This was not the first such disaster. There have been several other deadly incidents during the Hajj. The highest death toll was in 1990, when 1,426 people were killed in a stampede. The government needs to do what it can to avoid further disasters in the future.

HAJJ

Pilgrims on the Hajj first enter Makkah and circle the Ka'bah seven times. They run seven times between the hills of Safa and Marwah to remember Hagar's search for water for her thirsty infant, Ismail, the forefather of the Arab people. They visit the plains of Arafat, where the Prophet Muhammad preached his final sermon. At Mina, pilgrims throw stones at the pillars. At the end of the Hajj, people have a sheep slaughtered to remember how Ibraham killed a lamb in place of his son. This event is celebrated by Muslims worldwide at the festival of Id ul-Adha.

Thousands of pilgrims surround the Ka'bah at Makkah.

SAUDI ARABIA IS RULED BY THE SAUD FAMILY, *known as the House of Saud. The leading members of the royal family choose a king from amongst themselves. The current king, Abdullah Bin-Abd al-Aziz Al Saud, became head of state and prime minister in August 2005. He rules with the agreement of the rest of the royal family and the Council of Ulema, the religious leaders.*

There are no legal political parties, no parliament and no national elections in Saudi Arabia. The Crown Prince (the king-to-be) is always the deputy prime minister while the King appoints a Council of Ministers to form policies. These have to be in keeping with Islamic Sharia law, which also forms the basis of the justice system. The religious police enforce the rules among the public; they make sure women are covered in public and that men do not harass them, and check that people pray at the correct times.

PROGRESS

The government has started a programme of limited reforms to allow more people a say in government. It set up a Consultative Council in 1993 to review the government's decisions. Then, in 2005, the first nationwide municipal (city) elections were held. Voters were able to elect half the members of the municipal council while the other half were appointed by the government. Women were not allowed to vote but the election was seen as a turning point towards democracy.

A man votes in the 2005 municipal elections, the first held in Saudi Arabia.

 This Tornado aircraft of the Royal Saudi Air Force has been acquired as part of an ongoing arms deal with the UK.

DEFENCE POLICY

The Saudi government spends a vast amount of money on defence – about £12 billion ($20 billion) a year. There is evidence that the Kingdom has far more military equipment than its armed forces could possibly use. Some critics of the government believe that arms deals are often made for the benefit of members of the Saudi royal family, who receive money from foreign arms companies as a reward for making the deals. One of the biggest contracts is the Al-Yamamah deal with the UK, which began in 1985. It involves a series of arms sales to the

Kingdom, paid for in oil. In a later stage of the deal in 2005, the UK agreed to supply Saudi Arabia with fighter aircraft worth an estimated £6 billion ($10 billion).

GROUNDS FOR DEBATE

To many people, Saudi law seems barbaric. People can be flogged for minor offences, such as drunkenness. Convicted thieves may have their hand or foot cut off. Crimes that are considered the most serious are punished by public execution. Yet Saudis who defend Sharia law say that it is vital for keeping people safe and maintaining public order. It also protects business, as people can be put in prison for failing to pay debts. What do you think?

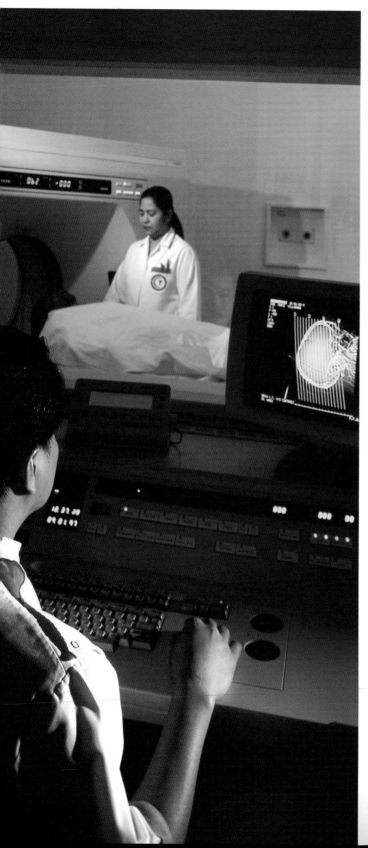

THE SAUDI ARABIAN ECONOMY IS EXTREMELY DEPENDENT ON THE OIL INDUSTRY. *After a slowdown in the mid-1980s and 1990s, the economy grew in the early 2000s, mainly because of high oil prices. There is a strong demand from Asia and the USA for Saudi oil, so Saudi Aramco is increasing its production. There has also been growth in other areas of the economy, especially banking, manufacturing and tourism.*

In recent years, the government has been able to use the high income from oil sales to pay off debts, fund education and development projects and raise welfare payments. More money has been devoted to security because of the threat of terrorism, and defence spending has risen.

DRAINS ON THE ECONOMY

However, the country still faces economic problems. There is high unemployment and fast population growth, which require increased government spending. Since 1980, the population has nearly tripled but in the same period of time, the income from oil in real terms (what can actually be bought with the money) has fallen by over 40 per cent. Another problem is that members of the Saud extended family – about 30,000 people – use a large proportion of the oil income. The percentage taken by the Sauds was fixed by King Faisal at 18 per cent but no one knows exactly how much they take because payments to the royal family are

Oil wealth has allowed Saudi Arabia to modernise rapidly. This includes buying state-of-the-art medical equipment, such as this scanner.

There is a wide variety of marine life living on the reefs of the Saudi Arabian Red Sea.

KNOW YOUR FACTS

Saudi Arabia is the world's largest exporter of oil. The petroleum sector accounts for about 75% of the revenue of the state, and oil accounts for 90% of earnings from exports. Saudi Arabia has around 80 oil and gas fields, but more than half of its reserves are contained in just 8 fields.

kept secret. However, there are around 7,000 princes, and even the least important ones are thought to receive at least £6,000 ($10,000) a month!

ENVIRONMENTAL ISSUES

Saudi Arabia faces great environmental challenges. The desert is spreading, mainly because of overgrazing. The Bedouin used to move around with their animals. Now, many live in settlements, so the animals graze in one place and eat up all the plants. Then the top layer of soil dries up and blows away. Over 30 per cent of grazing land has been

destroyed in this way. Regional governments are trying to protect the land. For example, they limit the size of herds that are allowed to graze in affected areas.

Another pressing issue is the overuse of underground water supplies. The government is investing vast sums in water desalination plants to remove the salt from seawater and provide an alternative source of water. About 60 per cent of water is already produced in this way.

SAUDI ARABIA HAS BEEN MUCH CRITICISED *for not respecting people's human rights. According to human rights organisations, people can be locked up without being told why. They are not allowed to contact anyone outside the prison. Prisoners are often tortured to force them to confess to a crime and many go on trial without a lawyer. The punishment could be flogging, amputation or even execution.*

Certain groups of people suffer particularly badly. Anyone who breaks the country's strict religious code can be arrested, as can migrant workers caught practising a faith other than Islam. Foreign workers can be deported for owning a symbol of their religion, such as a Bible. Shi'a Muslims from Saudi Arabia can only practise their faith in a limited way, and may be imprisoned for breaking the rules. People who campaign for reform can also be punished.

Women do not have equal rights to men (see page 14). Some migrant workers are badly exploited by their employers. They may be forced to work for over 12 hours a day, locked in their workplace and forbidden to speak to others. They often go hungry and unpaid.

A Saudi teacher and his class. Teachers in the Kingdom cannot discuss social issues.

GROUNDS FOR DEBATE

Allegations of human rights abuses in Saudi Arabia include judges imposing the death penalty on teenagers. According to the organisation Human Rights Watch, at the end of 2005 126 individuals were in prison facing execution for crimes they committed before they were 18 years old. Some were as young as 13 when they offended. Should Saudi judges have the power to treat young people as adults in cases where the death penalty may be imposed? What do you think?

SECRECY

There is no freedom of expression in the Kingdom. All political parties and trade unions are banned. The government censors the media and controls access to all forms of communication with the outside world, such as the Internet. There have been some reforms in education, but teachers still cannot have open discussions with their school students. For example, in November 2005, a court sentenced a high-school teacher to 40 months in prison and 750 whip lashes for talking to his students about current issues that affected their lives. They had discussed Christianity, Judaism and the dangers of terrorism.

A FAIR SYSTEM?

The Saudi government, however, states that the legal system is fair. It says that all prisoners have the right to a lawyer. The prisons are being updated – for example, Riyadh prison has exercise and entertainment facilities and a choice of food. All prisoners can be visited by their families. The death sentence is passed only on people who have committed violence against the community and it is possible to appeal against the judgement several times. The government is making efforts at reform. In 2005, the first-ever National Human Rights Association (NHRA) was formed; 10 of the 41 members were women.

Filipina workers on a Saudi street. Many migrant workers, particularly women, are treated badly by their employers.

KEY MOMENTS: FIRST GULF WAR

FOLLOWING THE END OF THE IRAN-IRAQ WAR IN 1988, *there was a dispute over land and oil rights between Kuwait and Iraq. It was not resolved. In August 1990, Iraqi ruler Saddam Hussein took matters into his own hands when he invaded and occupied Kuwait.*

Even though Saudi Arabia had supported Iraq during the Iran-Iraq War, the Kingdom feared it could be attacked by Iraq, too. Saudi Arabia was well armed but was not confident it could defeat Iraq

alone. So, King Fahd decided to invite US troops to defend his country. The USA was keen to help as it was concerned that oil-rich Saudi Arabia could fall into Iraqi hands.

Half-a-million US troops, with their planes, helicopters and tanks, rushed to the Kingdom. Their presence on holy Islamic soil caused great tension between the royal family and the public. The Council of Ulema, the religious leaders, had agreed to the measure reluctantly but they knew neither how many troops were coming, nor how long they would stay. King Fahd also brought in other Arab forces to fight alongside the Saudi ground troops. He helped provide supplies and accommodation for all his allies at a cost to his nation of between £33-37 billion.

A Saudi military convoy heads towards Kuwait during the first Gulf War.

Retreating Iraqi forces set Kuwait's oil wells on fire, causing huge damage.

IRAQ IS STRUCK

In January 1991 the allied forces, led by the USA and including Saudi fighter planes, unleashed massive bombing raids on Iraq. Iraq fired Scud missiles at Saudi Arabia, and for a few days occupied the Saudi border town of Khafji. Yet its forces could not match the might of the USA. In February, Iraq signed a truce. The Saudi people were horrified to see death and destruction in a neighbouring Arab country.

The consequences of Saudi involvement in the war were significant. It had been extremely costly, so the government had to cut back on public spending to pay off its debts. In addition, the USA still has an armed force in the Kingdom. This causes great ill-ease among the population and has probably fuelled the growth of the Islamic extremist movement, al-Qaeda.

KNOW YOUR FACTS

Days after Iraq invaded Kuwait, several Arab heads of state met to discuss an Arab solution to the dispute. Saddam Hussein accepted this could be possible. He withdrew 10,000 Iraqi troops from Kuwait and pulled back another 10,000 to the Iraqi border. Around the same time, US Secretary of Defense, Dick Cheney, met with King Fahd, and the Saudi king decided to invite US troops into the Kingdom. If King Fahd hadn't done this, the Arab states may have been able to reach a peaceful solution.

A videotape image of Saudi-born Osama Bin Laden speaking to his followers.

OSAMA BIN LADEN

In the 1980s, Saudi-born Bin Laden led a group of fighters in the struggle against the Soviet forces in Afghanistan. The Soviet army withdrew in 1989. When Iraq occupied Kuwait the following year, Bin Laden offered his forces to help defend Saudi Arabia. King Fahd rejected the offer, and shortly afterwards al-Qaeda was formed. In 1998 Osama Bin Laden announced there would be attacks on the USA and its allies.

AL-QAEDA AND SAUDI ARABIA

In the 1990s some moderate organisations campaigned for change in Saudi Arabia. By 2001 it was clear their influence had declined, and government opposition was increasingly led by radical Islamic groups, such as al-Qaeda. They believed the House of Saud was too friendly with Western governments and should be overthrown. Some Saudis

ON SEPTEMBER 11, 2001 THE WORLD REELED WITH SHOCK *when hijackers crashed two aeroplanes into the World Trade Center in New York. Another plane hit the Pentagon in Virginia and a total of almost 3,000 people lost their lives on this terrible day.*

The attacks were linked to the radical Islamic group, al-Qaeda, and Osama Bin Laden – widely seen as its leader. Out of the 19 suicide bombers, 15 were from Saudi Arabia.

KNOW YOUR FACTS

Al-Qaeda is made up of many independent cells, with common aims. They want US troops to leave Saudi Arabia, and US forces to leave the Middle East altogether. They wish for an end to the State of Israel because of its treatment of the mainly Muslim Palestinians. Their ultimate aim is to create Islamic governments across the Islamic world.

supported Bin Laden and his group's violent actions against the USA.

However, from May 2003, there were terrorist attacks within Saudi Arabia itself, including bomb attacks on US targets and the kidnapping and killing of foreign workers. Many ordinary Saudis agree with the aims to reduce US influence in their country but are outraged by al-Qaeda's violent tactics.

COUNTER-TERRORISM

Since the September 11 attacks, the Saudi government has brought in measures to prevent terrorism. It has arrested hundreds of al-Qaeda suspects and introduced strict banking controls so that suspected terrorist organisations cannot keep funds in the country.

GROUNDS FOR DEBATE

The number of US troops in Saudi Arabia was reduced to 500 by late 2004. Should the government listen to the demands of al-Qaeda and ask the US army to leave altogether? Alternatively, should tougher measures be brought in against the terrorists to close down their organisation?

▼ Since 9/11 many terrorist incidents, such as the bombings in London on 7 July 2005, have been linked to al-Qaeda.

EVEN THOUGH SAUDI ARABIA IS ONE OF THE WEALTHIEST COUNTRIES IN THE WORLD, *its wealth is unequally spread. In recent years, there has been a loss of goodwill towards the Saud family, which takes a large proportion of the oil riches. In addition, the Saudi government spends a huge amount on defence, which leaves less money for education and healthcare.*

UNEMPLOYMENT

The rapid population growth means there are not enough jobs. Each year about 300,000 young people enter the work force but there are only about 200,000 posts. The official figure for unemployment was 13 per cent of Saudi nationals in 2005. Unofficially, it is over 20 per cent.

Part of the problem lies in the school system, which does not prepare students adequately for the world of work. Teaching focuses on religious instruction and rote learning rather than independent thought. A survey of Riyadh high-school students in 2005 showed that fewer than one in six read for pleasure.

GROUNDS FOR DEBATE

Some believe that migrant workers – from highly skilled technical staff to street cleaners – should be replaced by native Saudis. Then Saudis would gain skills and not need to depend on foreign labour. But others argue that migrants have the right to move to another country to seek a better life. Even the lowest-paid Bangladeshis earn more in Saudi Arabia than they could at home.

Young men socialise in a café. With not enough jobs available, many young Saudi men are unemployed.

A Saudi father and his children. The birth rate is high in the Kingdom, and having seven children is not uncommon.

EMPLOYMENT

Another issue is the kind of job Saudis want. Many prefer not to take the low-paid routine jobs that migrants generally do. Since the 1980s, the government has tried to replace migrant workers with Saudis, with some success. Nowadays, there are Saudi salespeople and secretaries – but migrant workers still make up over half of the workforce.

For those in work, the average income fell dramatically from $25,000 per person in 1980 – similar to US levels – to $8,000 in 2003 (at current exchange rates: £15,000 to £4,800). This was mostly because of lower income from oil and rapid population growth.

The government cut spending on health and education and introduced higher taxes on electricity, petrol and telephone use. Fortunately, since 2003 the economic situation has improved, and spending on welfare has increased again.

However, there are still tensions in society. The terrorist actions have made people anxious. A growing drug problem among young people has fuelled an increase in crime, such as burglary, car theft and violent attacks. In general, Saudi Arabia can be a confusing place to grow up. It is a strict religious society, yet people have access to consumer goods, fast-food restaurants, the Internet and satellite TV.

 Some high-achieving women have obtained jobs such as television newsreaders for the Saudi TV channel, Akbaria.

SAUDI WOMEN'S LIVES CENTRE ON THE HOME.

Women are allowed in public but their lives are restricted. They have to wear an abaya, a black robe that covers the body, and cover their heads. They may not drive on public roads in cities.

Women cannot work, study or travel without the permission of a male relative. If they become divorced, their children stay with the father. According to Saudi custom, the purpose of these rules is to protect women from harm.

Girls have the same right to education as boys, although families don't always allow them to go to school. Women make up 55 per cent of university students but only 5 per cent of the workforce. Some have professional jobs as teachers, doctors, journalists or business managers, but are employed only to deal with other women. Few have a role in public life.

MOVES TOWARDS CHANGE

Customs are gradually changing. Since 2004, women have been allowed to carry out business activities without a male representative. A few Saudi women have entered the male world and become TV presenters and even pilots. To help ordinary women, some women-only projects are being set up to employ qualified staff. An Industrial Training Institute specially for females is being set up in Jeddah.

The Saud family has introduced some political reforms. When the Consultative Council was set up in 1993, three women were appointed to it, a step towards women's participation in politics. But women could not vote in the 2005 municipal elections.

At least the issue of women's rights is openly discussed now. The majority of Saudis think women should be allowed to drive freely. Awareness of the serious problem of violence against women has increased. In 2004, the well-known TV personality Rania al-Baz talked to the press after a severe beating by her husband. It is clear many Saudi women are working to improve their rights.

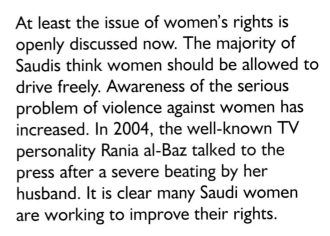

Hanadi Hindi became the first female pilot in Saudi Arabia in 2004.

GROUNDS FOR DEBATE

According to traditional Saudi thinking, a woman's main role is to care for the family. If women are allowed to drive and work outside the home alongside men, this will be harmful to the family unit. Mixing the sexes in schools and workplaces is against Islam. However, at a conference on women's issues in 2004, women argued that reform is needed to make society fairer to them. The court system and divorce laws are in men's favour. It is hard for women to find a job because of travel restrictions and the lack of suitable training. The women claimed it is not against Islam for women to be independent outside the home but against local traditions.
What do you think?

12 SAUDI ARABIA: WHAT'S IN STORE?

LOOKING AT THE ECONOMIC PROSPECTS, *Saudi Arabia will clearly remain dependent on selling oil, while continuing to develop other areas of the economy. The population is predicted to rise to 33 million by 2020. It will provide a growing market for goods and a challenge to the government to develop services for everyone. With ever-increasing numbers of Saudis looking for jobs, will the Kingdom continue to employ large numbers of foreign workers?*

Another vital issue is the relationship between Saudi Arabia and other countries. The Gulf region remains extremely unstable. The devastating war in Iraq has caused tens of thousands of deaths, and there are constant fears of

Despite rapid modernisation, Saudi culture remains strong. This picture shows a traditional wedding feast.

future conflict. The Saudi government has always relied on good relations with Europe and the USA for the defence of the Kingdom and for oil sales. Yet these links have caused anger and the growth of militant Islamic groups, which could threaten the government.

GROUNDS FOR DEBATE

There are many Muslim countries, such as Morocco, Jordan and Egypt, which hold elections, allow women freedom of movement, and permit different religious practices. They still have a Muslim identity. Some people argue this means that Saudi Arabia could reform without losing its Islamic character. Others say that the Saudi government is based on Sharia law as laid down in the Qur'an. It cannot be changed. What do you think?

 Inside a modern Saudi home. Satellite TV is officially banned, but this rule is generally ignored.

SAUDI SOCIETY

Saudi society is gradually opening up. Nowadays, people are discussing political reform – it is no longer taboo, a forbidden topic. In May 2005, three reformers who tried to set up a petition for an elected parliament were imprisoned for terms of between six and nine years. After King Abdullah took the throne a few months later, he freed them. It may be no longer a question of whether to reform, but when. There is growing press freedom, and articles about many of the problems of society now appear in the newspapers. Although there is censorship, many Saudis have links with the outside world. They can communicate on Internet chatrooms and mobiles.

At the moment, much of the decision making by the Sauds is shrouded in secrecy. Will they open up the workings of government to public view? Could the House of Saud ever share power with an elected parliament of men and women? It seems the Kingdom may have to find a way to balance traditional customs with reforms that allow more freedom. The multi-billionaire Prince Waleed expressed his view of the future: "Saudi Arabia westernised? Never! Modernised? Definitely!"

ce570: The Prophet Muhammad is born in Makkah.

1745: Muhammad Ibn Abd al-Wahhab, founder of an Islamic reform movement, joins with Saudi prince Muhammad Ibn Saud. They start to conquer parts of Arabia.

1902: Ibn Saud takes Riyadh and begins the struggle by the Sauds to regain control of the Arabian Peninsula.

1932: The Kingdom of Saudi Arabia is proclaimed under the rule of King Abd al-Aziz Al-Saud.

1938: Oil is discovered in the Kingdom.

1944: The Arabian American Oil Company (Aramco) is established.

1960: Saudi Arabia helps to form the Organisation of Petroleum Exporting Countries (OPEC).

1973: Saudi Arabia and other oil-producing countries stop selling oil to the USA for a short time because of its support for Israel in the Arab-Israeli War.

1975: King Faisal is assassinated. King Khalid is placed on the throne.

1979: Rebels occupy the Great Mosque in Makkah for two weeks.

1979–1980: Shi'a Muslims riot in eastern Saudi Arabia.

1980 Saudi Arabia takes full control of Aramco, renaming it Saudi Aramco.

1981: Saudi Arabia helps found the Gulf Cooperation Council, along with other Gulf countries.

1982: King Khalid dies, and Crown Prince Fahd becomes ruler.

1985: The Al-Yamamah arms deal is made with the UK.

1989: The Soviets withdraw from Afghanistan.

1990: A total of 1,426 pilgrims die in a stampede during the Hajj to Makkah.

1990: Iraq invades and occupies Kuwait. US forces are invited to Saudi Arabia to defend the Kingdom.

1991: A US-led Allied military operation, including Saudi air and land forces, defeats Iraq and forces it to withdraw from Kuwait.

1991: The USA makes a new arms deal with Saudi Arabia.

1993: The King sets up a Consultative Council of 60 people.

2001: Hijackers linked to al-Qaeda carry out deadly suicide attacks in the USA.

2003: Terrorist attacks begin within the Kingdom.

2004: Women are allowed to carry out business activities without a man to represent them.

2005:
March: National Human Rights Association is formed.

February to April: First municipal elections are held, and Islamic activists win.

August: Abdullah Bin Abd-al-Aziz Al-Saud becomes king.

December: The UK agrees a multi-billion pound deal to supply Saudi Arabia with Typhoon fighter jets.

2006:

January: Over 350 people die in a stampede during the Hajj.

BASIC FACTS

KINGDOM OF SAUDI ARABIA

LANGUAGE: Arabic

RELIGION: Islam

POPULATION: 26.4 million

CAPITAL: Riyadh

CURRENCY: Saudi Riyal (1 Saudi Riyal = US$27 approx)

MAJOR INDUSTRIES: Crude oil production, petroleum refining, basic petrochemicals (chemicals from petroleum and natural gas), other chemicals, cement, construction, fertiliser, plastics, commercial ship and aircraft repair.

MAIN NATURAL RESOURCES: Petroleum, natural gas, iron ore, gold, copper.

AGRICULTURAL PRODUCE: Wheat, barley, tomatoes, melons, dates, citrus fruits, mutton (from sheep), chickens, eggs, milk.

LIFE EXPECTANCY: 73 years (m) 78 years (f)

INTERNET DOMAIN: .sa

TIME ZONE GMT + 3

ADMINISTRATION: 13 provinces: Al-Bahah, Al-Hudud ash-Shamaliyah, Al-Jawf, Al-Madinah, Al-Qasim, Ar-Riyadh, Ash-Sharqiyah (Eastern Province), Asir, Ha'il, Jizan, Makkah, Najran, Tabuk

NEIGHBOURING COUNTRIES: Bahrain, Iraq, Jordan, Kuwait, Oman, Qatar, UAE, Yemen

EMPLOYMENT:

Agriculture 12%

Industry 25%

Services 63% (1999 estimate)

MAJOR INDUSTRIES: Crude oil production, petroleum refining, basic petrochemicals (chemicals from petroleum and natural gas), other chemicals, cement, construction, fertiliser, plastics, commercial ship and aircraft repair.

NATURAL RESOURCES: Petroleum, natural gas, iron ore, gold, copper.

AGRICULTURAL PRODUCE: Wheat, barley, tomatoes, melons, dates, citrus fruits, mutton (from sheep), chickens, eggs, milk.

Abaya A garment, usually black, that Saudi women wear over their clothes when they go out. It covers the whole body except the feet, face and hands.

Al-Qaeda A radical Islamic movement, prepared to use violence to achieve its aims. It has many groups worldwide.

Al-Yamamah A major on-going arms deal between the UK and the Saudi governments.

Amputation The cutting off of a body part. Under Sharia law, a hand can be amputated as a punishment for theft.

Bedouin This means "desert dweller" and refers to Arab nomads, who move from place to place with their herds.

Censor To check the material in the media, like books and newspapers, and remove anything that the government does not want people to know about.

Cold War The hostile relations between the countries allied to the Soviet Union and those allied to the USA during the period 1945 to 1990.

Consultative Council A group of advisers appointed by the king.

Death sentence A punishment passed in a law court that means the person convicted of the crime will be killed.

Desalination The process by which salt is removed from seawater to produce fresh water suitable for drinking.

Flogging A punishment in which a person is hit many times with a whip or a stick.

Overgrazing When herds of animals graze the plants in an area so heavily that the plants cannot grow back.

Peninsula An area of land that is almost surrounded by water but is joined to a larger piece of land.

Pentagon The headquarters of the US Department of Defense.

Qur'an The Muslim holy book, which Muslims believe was revealed to the Prophet Muhammad in the 7th century.

Salt flat An area of land covered in salt because the seawater that was there has dried up.

Scud missile A battlefield missile that Iraq adapted to have a greater range. Iraq fired a number of Scuds at Saudi Arabia and Israel during the 1991 first Gulf War.

Sharia law The Islamic law, which covers religious rituals and many aspects of daily life.

Soviet Belonging to the former USSR.

Suicide bombers People who carry out bomb attacks for political reasons. As well as blowing up other people, they blow themselves up in the attack.

WEBSITES

http://www.exploresaudiarabia.com/
An educational website with information about people and places, customs and culture, plus activities.

http://www.saudiembassy.net/
Official information provided by the Saudi Embassy in the USA, including news and information about the government, culture and economy.

http://www.amnesty.org/ailib/intcam/saudi/
Amnesty International's site about the Kingdom of Saudi Arabia.

http://hrw.org/doc?t=mideast&c=saudia
The Human Rights Watch site about Saudi Arabia.

www.cia.gov/cia/publications/factbook/geos/sa.html
Basic facts and figures about Saudi Arabia from the US Central Intelligence Agency.

www.lonelyplanet.com/worldguide/destinations/middle-east/saudi-arabia/
A travel guide with general information as well as details of places to see.

Note to parents and teachers:
Every effort has been made by the Publishers to ensure that the websites in this book are suitable for children, that they are of the highest educational value, and that they contain no inappropriate or offensive material. However, because of the nature of the Internet, it is impossible to guarantee that the contents of these sites will not be altered. We strongly advise that Internet access is supervised by a responsible adult.